# Max's book of Friends and strangers

to you lexie

## Contents



Nelson

# What is a friend?

A friend is someone
you know and like.

Think of some people

you know and like.

I know and like the lollipop man.

I see him every day

on my way to school.

I know and like my teacher.

She tells us lots of new things.

But she tells us off too!

I know and like the lady next door.

She has two children.

I go to play with them.

I know and like my friend and
his mum and dad.

I go to their house for tea
sometimes.

# What is a stranger?

A stranger is someone

you do not know.

Do not talk to people

you do not know.

Say NO to strangers.

Say NO to strangers.

## Quiz

Can you say? 

Who is the friend?

Who is the stranger?

We are friends!